The Essential Companion to Hadrian's Wall Path National Trail

Compiled by David McGlade

National Trail Manager

First edition published 2004 by the Hadrian's Wall Path Trust

ISBN: 0-9547342-0-3

Second edition published 2005 by the Countryside Agency

ISBN: 0-86170-692-7

Third edition published 2007 by Hadrian's Wall Heritage Limited

ISBN: 0-9547342-1-3

All rights reserved. No part of this publication may be reproduced, stored or introduced into a retrieval system, or transmitted, in any form or by any means (electronic, mechanical, photocopying, recording or otherwise), without the written permission of the owners of the copyright.

This book is sold subject to the condition that it shall not, by way of trade or otherwise, be lent, resold, hired out or otherwise, without the publisher's prior consent in any form of binding or cover other than that in which it is published and without a similar condition including this condition being imposed on the subsequent publishers

Copyright © Hadrian's Wall Heritage Limited

A large print version is available, contact the National Trail Manager, Hadrian's Wall Heritage Limited, East Peterel Field, Dipton Mill Road, Hexham, Northumberland, NE46 2 JT

Every effort has been made to check that the information in this guide is accurate at the time of going to print. The publishers cannot accept responsibility if opening times or arrangements are different to those advertised.

Cover photograph copyright © Roger Clegg

Printed on recycled stock. Designed by Differentia Ltd.

www.differentia.co.uk

Contents

Introduction	5
Helping us to look after Hadrian's Wall	7
Conservation tips	8
National Trail passport	12
Organisers of large groups or charity events	14
Top tips checklist	16
Frequently asked questions	19
Recommended publications	22
Map of Hadrian's Wall Path	26
Gradient profile	28
Distance charts	30
Using public transport	32
Secure car parking	38
Tide times on the Solway coast	40
Tourist Information Centres	42
Medical treatment	44
Historic sites, museums and visitor centres	47
Youth Hostels	53
Camping sites, barns and private hostels	55
Obtaining cash and paying for things	61
Water taps	67
WCs	71
Shops and Post Offices	74
Cafés (and other places where you will find refreshments)	82
Pub restaurants en route	89

Introduction

Welcome to the completely revised third edition of the Essential Companion to Hadrian's Wall Path National Trail. In it you will find details of all the everyday "basics" - the facilities and services that you will need to know about during your planning or when out on the Trail itself.

This guide was conceived in response to walkers' enquiries; where, for example, are the water taps, WCs and cash point machines, and what is the mobile phone reception like?

It attempts to paint as full a picture as possible but sometimes it points you in the direction of other sources of information; do send away, for example, for the leaflets and guides that we recommend in the publications section and check the National Trail website from time-to-time (www.nationaltrail.co.uk/hadrianswall) for the latest news and information.

When planning your walk, first look at the top tips and frequently asked questions - most of them are suggestions from walkers themselves. Then sit down with your walking companions, together with maps, guides and public transport information, and work out where you intend to be at the beginning and end of each day.

With good planning you will avoid the unnecessary gnashing of teeth that many unprepared walkers have experienced in the past. The buses connect with the Trail but you do need to study the timetables in order to avoid the prospect of another tiring trek at the end of an already long day's walk. Many a B&B owner has reported having to peel walkers, exhausted, off the ground - so take heed!

If you would like to recommend additional entries for next year's guide please make a note as you go along and let us know about them. Have a great walk!

All the lists in the guide work from east to west, that is, from Wallsend to Bowness-on-Solway

Helping us to look after Hadrian's Wall

Hadrian's Wall is a very sensitive place, a fragile piece of our heritage. Almost everywhere that you walk is archaeologically important, the many excavations have shown this to be the case, so we all have a responsibility to make sure that the surviving remains are preserved for future generations. Hadrian's Wall Path seeks to achieve an appropriate balance between the needs of recreation, conservation, economic development and farming.

When the National Trail received government approval for its creation it was decided that it should be managed as a green sward path. A green sward, or grass path, is important for three reasons. Firstly, by maintaining a healthy green surface and not damaging or breaking into it, any buried archaeological deposits will be protected. Secondly, it provides the most sympathetic setting possible for the Wall and its associated earthworks, and finally, most walkers will agree that a grass path is the most pleasant and comfortable of surfaces to walk upon.

This decision, supported by English Heritage, means that the management and marketing of Hadrian's Wall Path is different to that of recreational routes elsewhere in the UK. A grass path requires more intensive management compared with one that has been engineered; and understanding the dynamics of footfall, soil type, precipitation and drainage is as much an art as a science. In the wet winter months the soils become waterlogged and this is when the archaeology underfoot is especially vulnerable to damage. For this reason, the need to protect the very thing that people come from all over the world to visit, the National Trail is promoted as a spring, summer and autumn destination, but not as a winter one. We hope that you will understand, therefore, why our National Trail passport season runs only from the 1st May to the end of October each year. You can collect your passport stamps only within this period (see page 11).

By walking the Trail in the drier months, you will make a significant contribution to the well-being of the World Heritage Site. See its own code of respect, Every Footstep Counts (see page 9, also the Trail website www.nationaltrail.co.uk/hadrianswall). Please do your best to follow the code, by doing so everyone connected with the Wall will appreciate your help.

We do, of course, still welcome you to the region in the winter. Many of the Roman sites remain open, they are more robust and can better withstand visitor pressure; there are also many promoted circular walks where you will find the spirit of Hadrian's Wall Country. A leaflet summarizes all of the walks currently available, see the publications section on page 21-24.

Conservation tips

When out on the Trail there are a few very simple things that you can do that will not only help to conserve the historic landscape, but also protect farmers' grazing and give you a more pleasant surface to walk on. Everyone wins!

Tip number 1

You will come across small pictorial notices along the Trail that ask you to avoid walking in any worn lines in the grass, instead simply walk alongside them. If you are walking with someone or in a group please walk side-by-side instead of in single file.

Please keep off the wear line

Tip number 2

Keep to level ground and avoid the temptation to walk on anything that resembles a ridge. When the Trail was being designed the basic rule of thumb was to avoid as many of the lumps and bumps - earthwork archaeology - as possible. It generally tries to follow level ground and has been waymarked as such. Sometimes, however, you might be tempted to seek a better view by walking on an adjacent grassy ridge or a piece of raised ground but, if you do, you will almost certainly be walking on a sensitive archaeological earthwork.

P ease keep off the ridge

Tip number 3

Please resist the temptation to walk on Hadrian's Wall itself. The legal right of way is on the ground alongside the Wall and there is the added risk of injury from tripping on the uneven surface - every summer the local air ambulance has to rescue casualties from the Wall. Hadrian's Wall is also a fragile monument. The section rebuilt by John Clayton in the nineteenth century, still referred to as Clayton Wall, has almost no load bearing capacity and from time-to-time sections have collapsed. Please do your bit to help conserve the Wall for future generations by admiring it from alongside. Thank you.

Every Footstep Counts

The World Heritage Site's very own country code

(The code is also on the Trail's website - www.nationaltrail. co.uk/hadrianswall). All of the organisations associated with the care and management of Hadrian's Wall World Heritage Site have signed up to the following code. Please do your bit to help them protect it for future generations.

- The risk of erosion to this historic monument is at its greatest during wet winter conditions, particularly between November and April. Alternative circular walks close to the Wall have been specifically designed and are advisable during these times. They allow walkers to experience the stunning and dramatic scenery of the World Heritage Site whilst preserving the Wall, its earthworks and surrounding environment.

- Start and finish your walk along the Wall at different places, or follow a circular route. Details of some of the huge range of walks are listed in the leaflet Walking Around Hadrian's Wall (which also contains this code - see page 23). Allow extra time to visit the Roman forts and museums and other attractions in Hadrian's Wall Country. Information on all walks, attractions, accommodation and events is available from the Hadrian's Wall Information Line (telephone 01434 322002).

- Please don't climb or walk on top of Hadrian's Wall.
- Camping is allowed on official sites only.
- Support people living and working in the World Heritage Site by staying nearby, and use local shops, restaurants and pubs. You will be most welcome and will get a real flavour of the area.
- Take any litter away with you and never light fires.
- Close all gates behind you, unless it is clear that the farmer needs the gate to be left open.
- Keep to paths signed from the road with coloured arrows or the National Trail acorn symbol.
- Please keep your dog under close control, in fields with sheep this means on a lead. On National Trust property it is compulsory to keep your dog on a lead.

National Trail passport

Between May and October each year, collect all six stamps in the passport from the stamping stations to qualify for the exclusive Hadrian's Wall Path completion badge and certificate. Purchase the badge (£2.95) from either Segedunum Roman Fort in Wallsend or the King's Arms in Bowness-on-Solway or by mail order from the Hadrian's Wall Information Line. Send completed passports and a cheque for £2.95 (made payable to Tynedale Council) to: Haltwhistle Tourist Information Centre, Railway Station, Station Road, Haltwhistle, NE49 9HN. Tel: 01434 322002.
Email haltwhistletic@btconnect.com

Segedunum Roman Fort - start of Trail. Situated inside main entrance of the museum. Available normal opening hours (see list of historic sites).

TOTAL petrol garage. 150 yards east of Segedunum. Open Mon - Fri 07.00 to 21.00; Sat 07.00 to 20.00; Sun 08.00 to 20.00.

Robin Hood Inn - 1 mile (1.3 km) west of Whittledene Reservoir. Grid Ref NZ 050 684. Situated on right hand side of porch entrance. Available anytime.

Chesters Roman Fort - (Chollerford) Grid Ref NY911 704. Situated inside main entrance of museum. Available standard English Heritage opening hours. When site is closed an outside stamping box will be displayed at the entrance to the car park.

Birdoswald Roman Fort - Grid Ref NY615 663. Situated inside main entrance and shop. Available normal opening hours. When site is closed an outside stamping box will be displayed on the site building.

Sands Sports Centre - Carlisle. Grid Ref NY402 565. Situated inside centre café - access via glass door from Trail on riverside path. If locked, access at front of building. Available during normal opening hours.

The Banks Promenade (or the King's Arms) - Bowness-on-Solway. Grid Ref NY223 628. Situated at the very end of the Trail. Available any time. Available at the King's Arms during normal opening hours.

Organisers of large groups or charity events

If you are organising a walk for a large group or for a charity event the following tips are for your guidance. The advice attempts to strike a balance between our need to manage and conserve the Trail and World Heritage Site, and your desire for an enjoyable walk.

1. The National Trail project cannot offer you a guiding service. If you require an experienced guide please consider one of the walking operators listed in the Hadrian's Wall Country Mini Guide. (See Publications: page 23).

2. It is vital that you familiarise yourself with the Trail long before the actual event. Do be aware of the terrain and think about the abilities of your walkers. Many groups either underestimate the difficulty of the walk or overestimate their own abilities.

3. Please plan your walk for the drier months of the year, between May and October. Avoiding the wet winter months will help to prevent erosion to both the Trail and monument. (See page 6).

4. Do let the National Trail Manager know that you are planning an event. You will be given as much advice and help as possible.

5. A party of 50 is considered to be a reasonable size for an event walk; during the peak summer season larger groups may encounter parking congestion at

some places used as check points. Remember that your large group may not be the only one on the Trail at any one point in time.

6. Note that there is absolutely nowhere to park in either Port Carlisle or Bowness-on-Solway. Taking a coach into the latter has, in the past, caused chaos there.

7. Be aware of where all the WCs, water taps and other facilities are. Please avoid knocking on private occupiers' doors to ask for water.

8. Read the top-tips section for good general advice!

Top tips - check list

Most of the following tips and suggestions have been suggested by Trail walkers themselves; they should stand you in good stead for your walk along the National Trail. (Any further tips for future editions will be gratefully received!).

1. Book your accommodation beforehand. If you turn up without a booking during the main season you risk being disappointed.

2. Carry a cheque book. Very few of the small accommodation addresses accept debit and credit cards. Also, plan ahead and note where the many banks, cash point machines, Post Offices and shops that provide a cash-back service are. (See page 74).

3. It is not an easy walk. Some guidebook and magazine articles have described it as "not a challenge walk", but neither is it a stroll in the park. The section between Chollerford and Birdoswald, some 23 miles and for the most part a switchback with seemingly endless ups and downs, usually sorts out the fit from the un-fit.

4. Know where you can access public transport and carry the necessary timetables.

5. The quietest time for visitors during the summer is outside of the school holidays. This means avoiding the last week of July, all of August and the first week of September.

6. In the interests of conserving the Path and ancient monument, the best time to walk the Trail is from May to October. This is the time when the ground is normally drier and able to withstand the pressure of thousands of pairs of feet. The Trail passport also operates only during this period. (See page 11).

7. Note that the seasonal AD 122 Hadrian's Wall bus operates a daily service, connecting the Trail with many of the nearby towns and villages. Send away for the public transport guide. (See page 23).

8. When booking accommodation check to see if a pick-up and drop-off service is provided.

9. Most people begin their holiday on a Saturday or Sunday. By starting on a weekday you will avoid some of the crowds and find it easier to book your accommodation.

10. Carry your mobile 'phone with you. Use it to telephone ahead to order your bait (Geordie and Cumbrian for packed lunch) from the many cafés or to meet your pre-arranged pick-ups. The signal is sometimes weak between about Birdoswald and Walton in Cumbria, also around Chollerford in Northumberland.

11. The occasional Internet facility along the Trail is useful for checking the weather forecast, and for 12 below (check the other lists for Internet cafés and other Internet access).

12. Make sure that you know when the Solway marshes are likely to be subject to tidal flooding. (See page 40).

13. If you use the Tyneside Metro have change ready for the ticket machines, there are no ticket offices at the stations.

14. The route is very exposed to the sun and there is very little shade to be had. Carry a hat and sun screens.

15. If you are a member of either English Heritage or the National Trust don't forget to pack your membership cards; several of the historic sites in the area belong to the organisations.

16. Midges can sometimes be a problem! Carry a suitable insect repellent.

17. The 12 miles on Tyneside are on Tarmac paths that can be unforgiving on your feet. You might prefer to wear soft shoes or trainers for this section. In any case carry a blister repair kit.

18. Don't forget to pack your map and/or guidebook!

Frequently asked questions

How long is the Trail? The Trail is 84 miles, or 135 kilometres, long.

How long is the Wall? Don't confuse this with the length of the Trail. The Wall is 73 miles (80 Roman miles) long. A Roman mile is 1620 yards.

East or west - which is the best way to walk? Eastbound walkers start on the quiet Solway estuary and finish in the bustling city, westbound walkers do it the other way around. It is, of course, a matter of opinion, however, the National Trail Manager's personal preference (having walked it in both directions) is to start in Wallsend and head west. Many walkers agree, an often-heard comment is that the landscape "gets better" the further west you go. Certainly, the peace, solitude and expansive views across the Solway Firth presents a very agreeable end to a long journey.

What about the prevailing wind? We are often asked about this and whether it is better to walk with it on your back instead of in your face. In the peak summer months it really shouldn't influence your decision because then the wind is normally fairly benign.

How many days should we take? If you are used to walking for several days at a time, then six should be enough. If, however, you are less experienced you should build more time into your schedule or you may find it difficult to fit in visits to the Roman Wall sites.

Are there enough campsites? The provision of campsites has improved but the chain is still incomplete. The new camping barns, private hostels and youth hostels are useful for filling in the gaps. We do ask you, however, not to wild camp, it causes problems for both Trail staff and farmers.

Is it easy to follow? The Trail is clearly signed, and waymarked with the standard National Trail acorn symbol and waymark arrows.

On Tyneside, why is it called Hadrian's Way? This is the local name for what was originally a city cycleway. The name simply stuck so the Trail project decided to leave things the way they were. It is, however, still signed with the acorn symbol.

What are the best publications? See page 21.

Latitude and Longitude?

Segedunum Roman Fort at Wallsend:

Latitude 54°: 59": 18' north

Longitude 1°: 31": 51' west

Bowness-on-Solway:

Latitude 54°: 57": 13' north

Longitude 3°: 12": 44' west

Are there any walking operators? There are several firms that arrange accommodation, guided and self-guided itineraries along the Trail. A full list of operators is to be found in the Hadrian's Wall Country Mini Guide. (See pages 82 to 86 of the guide).

Is there a baggage handling service? Some of the walking operators will arrange to move your bags for you each day. There are three firms providing a service for the independent traveller.

The Walkers' Baggage Transfer Company, which can be contacted at Tel: 0870 990 5549. Fax: 0870 443 0135. Operates all year. www.walkersbags.co.uk

The Sherpa Van Project. Operates daily from April to October, 09.00 to 20.00. Out of season Mon-Fri 09.00 to 17.00. Sat 10.00 to 14.00. Contact 0871 520 0124. Fax 01748 825561 www.sherpavan.com

Hadrian's Haul operates all year. Pick ups/drop offs available as required between Wallsend and Bowness and beyond. Contact 07967 564823 or Email info@hadrianshaul.com

Is there much road walking? No, but do take care at the road crossings. There are several crossings across the busy B6318 between Heddon-on-the-Wall and Chollerford. Also take care crossing the A6071 at Newtown in Cumbria.

Is it very hilly? In places yes - see our helpful gradient profile on pages 28 and 29. The interpretation panels along the way provide more useful information about the Trail together with topical and historic details.

Recommended publications

The Trail itself

Before you start planning your visit to Hadrian's Wall Path you will need a map or guidebook. At the moment we recommend two publications, the official Aurum Press guidebook and the excellent Harvey strip map. Both will escort you along the Trail but which one you decide to use is a matter of choice, some walkers carry both. The guidebook is a detailed description of the route with Ordnance Survey strip maps at 1:25,000 scale while the Harvey map is at 1:40,000 scale with some sections enlarged for additional clarity. It also includes some helpful interpretive information.

You might prefer a set of four Ordnance Survey maps; they have the advantage of showing the Wall and Trail in their wider context.

Hadrian's Wall Path by Tony Burton (2003); Aurum Press. £12.99. ISBN 978 1 84513 285 9.

Hadrian's Wall (2003); strip map by Harvey. £9.95. ISBN 1 85137 405 1.

Hadrian's Wall Path. Two-way National Trail description by Mark Richards (2004); Cicerone. £12.95. ISBN 1 85284 392 6. The book pays attention to the sustainable use of the Trail and the care of sensitive archaeological areas.

Ordnance Survey maps. Four Explorer map sheets at 1:25,000 scale are necessary for the Trail, at £7.99 each, as follows: 314 (Solway); 315 (Carlisle); Explorer sheets 316 (Newcastle); plus the Explorer (OL) 43 (Hadrian's Wall).

Background reading

If you would like to read around the history and archaeology of Hadrian's Wall we recommend the following:

Ancient Frontiers - Exploring the geology and landscape of the Hadrian's Wall area (2006); British Geological Survey. £8.00. ISBN 0 8527 2541 8.

Hadrian's Wall by David Breeze and Brian Dobson (2000); Penguin. £9.99. ISBN 0 14027 1821.

Hadrian's Wall by David Breeze (2006); English Heritage. £4.99. ISBN 978 1 85074 979 0. This is the third edition of this popular souvenir guide, updated and lavishly illustrated.

Other walking guides

Walking in Britain by David Else et al (2007); Lonely Planet. £14.99. ISBN 978 1 74104 202 3. New revised edition; ideal for planning trips to the Wall and beyond in the region.

The Roman Ring. by Mark Richards (2006); Shepherd's Walks. £9.99. ISBN 0 9552624 0 2. (Dedicated to John Clayton, pre-eminent in the early conservation movement). An alternative option to the Trail, two routes that form a ring around the central section of the Wall; includes several shorter circular walks on and around the Trail.

'Must get' information

Send away to the Hadrian's Wall Information Line (01434 322002; email haltwhistletic@btconnect.com) for the following free guides:

- The Hadrian's Wall Country Mini Guide including Walking and Cycling Accommodation;
- Hadrian's Wall Bus AD122 2007 Bus & Rail Timetable;
- Walking around Hadrian's Wall - this leaflet highlights the promoted circular walks within Hadrian's Wall country. It also contains Every Footstep Counts, the World Heritage Site's code of respect.

Recommended bookshops

For a reliable service we recommend that you consider using one of the following:

1. For mail order telephone sales (credit and debit cards) contact the Hadrian's Wall Information Line on 01434 322002. Address: Haltwhistle TIC, Railway Station, Station Road, Haltwhistle, Northumberland, NE49 0AH. Email haltwhistletic@btconnect.com
2. For Internet sales contact the Offa's Dyke Centre Internet Bookshop. For many years the Offa's Dyke Centre has served the needs of walkers using the Offa's Dyke Path National Trail. It now sells guidebooks for all of England and Wales' National Trails via a secure Internet facility (www.offasdyke.demon.co.uk).

Address: The Offa's Dyke Centre, West Street, Knighton, Powys, LD7 1EN   Telephone: 01547 528753. Email oda@offasdyke.demon.co.uk

Useful websites

www.nationaltrail.co.uk/hadrianswall

www.hadrians-wall.org

www.yha.org.uk

www.independenthostelguide.co.uk

www.nationaltrust.org.uk

www.english-heritage.org.uk

www.metoffice.gov.uk

www.ramblers.org.uk

Hadrian's Wall Path National Trail

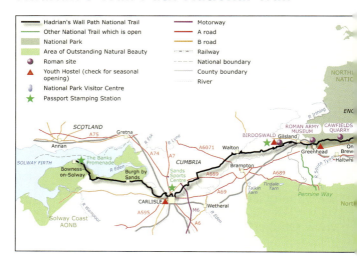

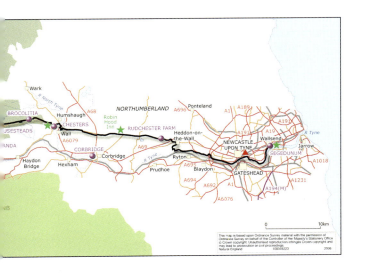

Gradient Profile

Below are three gradient profiles showing the Hadrian's Wall Path as it stretches coast-to-coast across the country. Along the way you will find more detailed information on the interpretation panels situated at strategic points. The panels provide details of the route, maps and locations of nearby towns and settlements as well as an interpretation

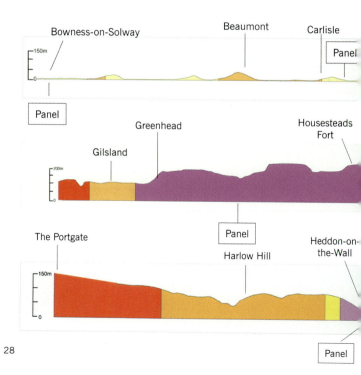

of the landscape, nature and heritage of the area. We hope that they will help newcomers to the Trail to get a feel for what is ahead of them. The panels' locations are indicated on the profiles.

Key

- **Easy walk** — Suitable for wheelchair users.
- **Easy walk** — Unsuitable for wheelchair users.
- **More difficult walk** — Wear boots.
- **Very strenuous walk** — Especially in poor weather.

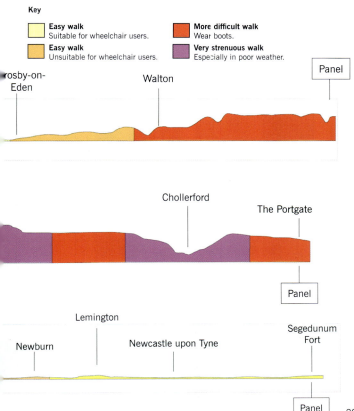

Distance Calculator (miles)

	Wallsend	Tyne bridge	Heddon	A68 Errington Arms	Chollerford	Housesteads	Steel Rigg	Greenhead	Gilsland	Walton	Newtown	Crosby	Carlisle	Burgh by Sands	Bowness
Wallsend															
Tyne bridge	5														
Heddon	15	10													
A68 Errington Arms	25	20	10												
Chollerford	30	25	15	5											
Housesteads	39	34	24	15	10										
Steel Rigg	42	37	27	18	13	3									
Greenhead	49	44	34	24	19	10	7								
Gilsland	51	46	36	26	21	12	9	2							
Walton	58	53	43	33	29	20	17	10	8						
Newtown	60	55	45	35	30	22	19	12	10	2					
Crosby	65	60	50	40	36	27	24	17	15	7	5				
Carlisle	70	65	55	45	40	32	29	22	20	12	10	5			
Burgh-by-Sands	77	72	62	52	47	38	36	29	27	19	17	12	7		
Bowness	84	79	69	59	55	46	44	37	35	27	25	20	15	8	

Distance Calculator (kilometers)

	Wallsend	Tyne bridge	Heddon	A68 Errington Arms	Chollerford	Housesteads	Steel Rigg	Greenhead	Gilsland	Walton	Newtown	Crosby	Carlisle	Burgh by Sands	Bowness
Wallsend															
Tyne bridge	8														
Heddon	24	16													
A68 Errington Arms	40	32	16												
Chollerford	48	40	24	8											
Housesteads	63	55	39	24	16										
Steel Rigg	67	59	43	29	21	5									
Greenhead	79	71	55	39	31	16	11								
Gilsland	82	74	58	42	34	20	15	3							
Walton	93	85	69	53	47	32	27	16	13						
Newtown	96	88	72	56	46	35	30	19	16	3					
Crosby	104	96	80	64	58	43	39	27	24	12	8				
Carlisle	112	104	88	72	64	51	46	35	32	19	16	8			
Burgh-by-Sands	123	115	99	83	75	61	58	46	43	30	27	19	11		
Bowness	135	126	110	94	88	74	70	59	56	43	40	32	24	13	

Using public transport

Hadrian's Wall Path must rank as one of the easiest of National Trails to get to. It is served by two regional cities, Carlisle (in the west) and Newcastle upon Tyne (to the east), both of which have inter-city rail links and National Express coach services. Newcastle itself has its own international airport with scheduled services to many UK and overseas destinations.

Once you have arrived, moving between the two main centres along the Trail is straight forward although timing is important and you must plan ahead. Don't assume that buses will serve every access point to the Trail because you will be disappointed. Please bear in mind that the frequency of service, and sometimes the service itself, varies according to the time of year. **The AD 122 Hadrian's Wall bus service**, for example, operates a daily service between early April and late October, connecting the Trail to the main towns and villages where most of the B&B accommodation is to be found. Outside of this season you will find it more difficult to plan your itinerary.

Arriving in Newcastle:

By air

Newcastle airport couldn't be more convenient for the start of your holiday. You are quickly through baggage reclaim and passport control and onto the Tyne and Wear Metro which has its own airport station. The Metro is a modern, frequent and reliable service but the stations are not staffed and tickets are purchased from a machine. Not every Metro station has a change machine so a **top tip** is to have change ready.

By ferry

For anyone arriving from Holland or Scandinavia the way to the National Trail from the Royal Quays ferry terminal is straightforward. To go into Newcastle take the special DFDS ferry bus direct to Central Station. The station is a useful hub to orientate yourself around Newcastle with the city's youth hostel, for example, only three Metro stops away (for which you should alight at Jesmond Metro).

To go to the start of the National Trail at Wallsend you will need to take a local bus service (317) from outside the Wet 'n' Wild leisure complex for the 20 minute journey to Wallsend Metro station. The start of the Trail at Segedunum Roman Fort is then only a three minute walk away.

By train

This couldn't be easier. Newcastle is served by the East Coast Main Line with frequent GNER services from London King's Cross, Edinburgh and Glasgow. For telephone bookings: 08457 225 225. www.gner.co.uk

Virgin Cross Country also connects Newcastle with Edinburgh, the south coast of England, and Wales. For telephone bookings: 08457 222 333. www.virgin.com/trains

Another important regional service into Newcastle is by First Trains with its Trans Pennine Express service from

Liverpool, Manchester and Leeds. For more information see: www.firstgroup.com/tpexpress

Arriving in Carlisle:

By train

Carlisle is served by the West Coast Main Line with frequent Virgin Trains from Glasgow, London Euston and the south. Contact details as above.

Coach travel

National Express Coaches serve both Newcastle (St James' Boulevard - five minutes' walk from Central Station) and Carlisle (bus station in Lonsdale Street). For telephone bookings: 08705 808080. www.nationalexpress.com

Leaving Newcastle:

By ferry

To return to the Royal Quays ferry terminal take the DFDS ferry bus that leaves outside Central Station only. It departs at 3pm and 4:15pm.

Traveline

The national public transport information line is 0870 608 2 608 or visit www.traveline.org.uk

National Rail enquiries

National Rail enquiry service: 08457 484950 or visit www.nationalrail.co.uk

Travelling around the World Heritage Site

The Hadrian's Wall Information Line will send you the Hadrian's Wall Bus AD 122 leaflet; contains AD122 and other bus and railway timetables.
(haltwhistletic@btconnect.com or tel 01434 322002)

AD 122 Hadrian's Wall bus

The route, with other interim stops, can be used to connect Newcastle; Heddon-on-the-Wall; Errington Arms (A68); Corbridge; Hexham; Chesters Roman Fort, Chollerford; Housesteads Roman Fort; Once Brewed National Park Visitor Centre; Vindolanda Roman Fort; Milecastle Inn near Cawfields; Haltwhistle; Roman Army Museum at Walltown; Greenhead; Gilsland; Birdoswald Roman Fort; Lanercost Priory; Brampton; Crosby-on-Eden; Carlisle; Kirkandrews; Beaumont; Burgh by Sands; Bousted Hill; Drumburgh; Glasson; Port Carlisle and Bowness-on-Solway. One, three and seven-day tickets are available on the bus, also from Tourist Information Centres. Guides travel on the bus daily (check timetable).

685 bus service between Carlisle and Newcastle

Connects Newcastle with Heddon-on-the-Wall; Corbridge; Hexham; Haydon Bridge; Haltwhistle; Greenhead; Brampton and Carlisle.

93, 71 bus services between Carlisle and Bowness-on-Solway

An important local service for getting in and out of Bowness. The service connects Carlisle with Kirkandrews;

Beaumont; Burgh-by-Sands; Bousted Hill; Drumburgh; Glasson; Port Carlisle and Bowness-on-Solway.

880 bus service between Hexham, Wark and Bellingham

Useful if you want to travel between Hexham; Acomb; Wall; Chollerford; Humshaugh; Wark; and Bellingham.

185 bus service between Carlisle and Housesteads Roman Fort

Connects Carlisle with Brampton; Gilsland; Roman Army Museum at Walltown; Haltwhistle. For the last service of the day it also stops at Once Brewed National Park Visitor Centre and Housteads Roman Fort before returning to Carlisle.

Tyne Valley Railway Line

Regular trains connect Newcastle with Wylam; Prudhoe; Corbridge; Hexham; Haydon Bridge; Bardon Mill; Haltwhistle; Brampton and Carlisle. (Not every station is served by every service).

Other services

94, 97 bus services out of Carlisle:

With careful planning it is possible to get to or from Walton or Newtown using this bus service. Request a timetable from Traveline.

Taxis

Go to www.traintaxi.co.uk for details of taxi services

available from the railway stations between Tyneside and Carlisle. Traintaxi lists all the train, metro, tram and underground stations in Britain and lists up to three local taxi or minicab firms serving each station.

Secure car parking

If you arrive by car you will want to leave it somewhere that is as safe as possible. Sometimes hotels will oblige but if you need to use a car park you will generally find it easier to find space in Newcastle where there is more capacity. In any case it is advisable to pre-book. Please also make a special note that there is absolutely nowhere for day visitors to park in Bowness-on-Solway. (See below for long-stay parking in Bowness). The following places have been recommended.

Newcastle airport

You don't have to travel by air to use the airport's secure long-stay car parking facility. The airport is easily accessed from the A1, and the Metro journey back into Newcastle city centre takes only 25 minutes. A week's car parking costs around £40 although Co-op Travelcare sometimes has discounted offers. Contact the Prudhoe branch for the latest deals, telephone 01661 836800.

Royal Quays ferry terminal

If arriving by ferry there is a long-stay secure car park at the ferry terminal, ask your travel agent for details.

Carlisle railway station

You can leave your car at the station for up to five days; the current charge is £6 per day, payable at the meter.

Bowness-on-Solway

Parking on private property by arrangement.
Telephone 016973 51788.

Wallsend Rectory, B&B, Bowness, private grounds. Telephone 016973 51055. Charge is £1.50 per day for guests either starting or ending the trail or £3 for non guests per day. Limited availability, please telephone to book.

The Old Chapel. Telephone 016973 51126. Grid Ref NY224627. Car parking available by prior agreement. Also café, group accommodation and shop. www.oldchapelbownessonsolway.com

Tide times for the Solway coast

The Solway coast between Dykesfield and Drumburgh, also between Port Carlisle and Bowness-on-Solway is at sea level. These areas can be affected by tidal flooding. You must be aware of when this is likely to occur and allow sufficient time for a safe walk. Information is provided for your benefit in two ways.

Notice boards - Located at Dykesfield and Bowness-on-Solway. The boards contain the current month's tide prediction tables.

The Internet - The UK Hydrographic Office provides a free seven day prediction service and you can access it any time by going to www.ukho.gov.uk then proceed as follows:

select: Easy Tide

select: Click for FREE predictions for today and the next 6 days

select: Search

select: Search for Silloth

select: Predict

select: Predict

You will then see a seven day tide prediction forecast table. You are interested in high tides with heights of 9 metres and above which may cause the affected parts of the Trail to flood.

However, because the prediction is for the nearest port of Silloth you will need to do a conversion for the Trail as follows:

1. during Greenwich Mean Time (also known as winter time) add on one hour;
2. during British Summer Time add on two hours.

You will now have a time for high tide adjusted for the Trail. **Finally, allow for an hour either side of high tide when the sections affected should be avoided.**

Do bear in mind that the tide tables give predictions only and that many conditions, for example wind speed and atmospheric pressure, can influence the likelihood of the Solway marshes flooding. The Solway estuary can look an entirely benign place, but the water can rise very quickly.

Tourist Information Centres (TICs)

(open all your unless otherwise stated.)

Tyneside and Northumberland

8-9 Central Arcade, Market Street, Newcastle upon Tyne, NE1 5BQ. Telephone: 0191 277 8000. Internet access.

The Guildhall Visitor Centre, Riverside Entrance, Quayside, Newcastle upon Tyne, NE1 3AF. Next to the Swing Bridge. Telephone as above. Internet access.

Hill Street, Corbridge, Northumberland NE45 5AA. Telephone: 01434 632815. Open Easter to October.

Wentworth Car Park, Hexham, Northumberland NE46 1QE. Telephone: 01434 652220.

Once Brewed, Northumberland National Park Visitor Centre, Military Road, Bardon Mill, Hexham, Northumberland NE47 7AN.

Telephone: 01434 344396. Open daily to 31st October. November to March weekends only. Internet access.

Haltwhistle. Railway Station, Station Road, Haltwhistle, Northumberland. NE49 0AH. Telephone: 01434 322002. Haltwhistle TIC is also the Hadrian's Wall Information Line.

Cumbria

The Moot Hall, Market Place, Brampton, Cumbria CA8 1RW.

Telephone: 01697 73433. Open Easter to October.

Old Town Hall, Green Market, Carlisle, Cumbria CA3 8JE. Telephone: 01228 625600.

Medical treatment

The 24 hour NHS Direct telephone help-line is 0845 4647. The service is staffed by nurses and you can call for immediate advice if you or a family member feels ill. Your accommodation address should also be able to advise you of local GP and dentist surgeries.

Hospitals close to Hadrian's Wall:

Emergencies

In an emergency dial 999 or 112.

Newcastle General Hospital,

Westgate Road, Newcastle upon Tyne.

Telephone: 0191 233 6161.

Hexham General Hospital,

Corbridge Road, Hexham.

Telephone: 01434 655655.

Haltwhistle War Memorial Hospital,

Westgate, Haltwhistle.

Telephone: 01434 320225. 24-hour, minor injuries only.

Brampton War Memorial Hospital,

Tree Road, Brampton.

Telephone: 016977 2534.

Open only 08.00 to 20.00. Minor injuries only.

The Cumberland Infirmary,

Newtown Road, Carlisle.
Telephone: 01228 523444.

Pharmacies

The following are the pharmacies that we consider to be the most useful for walkers:

Wallsend

Boots Chemist. The Forum. Telephone: 0191 262 3673. Open: Mon-Fri 09.00 to 17.30. Sat: 09.00 to 17.30.

Newcastle

Boots Chemist. Hotspur Way, Eldon Square, Newcastle upon Tyne, NE1 7XE.Telephone: 0191 232 9844. Open: Mon, Wed, Fri, Sat: 08.30-1800. Tues: 08.45-18.00. Thur: 08.30-20.00. Sun: 11.00-17.00.

Wylam

Wylam Pharmacy. Main Road. Telephone: 01661 852253. Open: Mon - Fri: 08.30 to 18.00. Sat: 09.00 to 12.00.

Corbridge

Henderson's Pharmacy. Town Hall Building, Princes Street. Telephone: 01434 632046. Open: Mon - Fri: 09.00 to 18.00. Sat: 09.00 to 16.00.

Hexham

Pattinson's Pharmacy. Fore Street. Tel: 01434 603080. Open: Mon, Tues, Wed, Fri: 08.45 to 17.15. Thurs, Sat: 08.45 to 16.00.

Haltwhistle

Alliance Pharmacy. Eden House, Westgate. Telephone: 01434 320511. Open: Mon - Fri: 09.00 to 18.00. Sat: 09.00 to 13.00.

Brampton

H. Jobson. Market Place. Telephone: 016977 2501. Open: Mon-Fri: 09.00 to 17.30. Sat: 09.00 to 17.00.

Carlisle

Boots Chemist. 43 English Street. Telephone: 01228 542944.

Open: Mon-Wed: 08.30 to 17.45. Thurs: 08.30 to 19.00. Fri, Sat: 08.30 to 17.45. Sun: 11.00 to 17.00.

Historic sites, museums and visitor centres

This list includes the Roman sites and museums, other historic sites, attractions and visitor centres close to the Trail. When helpful, OS Grid References are given, otherwise distance or brief directions from the Trail. For full details refer to the relevant web sites or organisation membership handbooks. There are, of course, many other attractions in places like Newcastle, your suggestions for next year's guide are welcome. The tourist information centres are listed separately.

Tyneside and Northumberland

South Shields

Arbeia Roman Fort. Telephone 0191 456 1369. Not on the Trail but well worth a visit. 15 minutes' walk from South Shields Metro. Site free but charge for entry to award winning Time Quest - hands on archaeology display. Open: 1st April to 31st October, Mon - Sat 10.00 to 17.30; Sun 13.00 to 17.00. From 1st November to 31st March, Mon-Sat 10.00 to 15.30. Closed Sunday. Time Quest hours vary, please check.
www.twmuseums.org.uk

Bede's World. Telephone 0191 489 2106. Not on the Trail but well worth a visit. 20 minutes' walk from Bede Metro station. Anglo-Saxon demonstration farm and museum with permanent exhibition. Admission charge. Open: April-Oct, Mon-Sat 10.00 to 17.30; Sun 12.00

to 17.30; Nov-March, Mon-Sat 10.00 to 16.30; Sun 12.00 to 16.30. (Last admission to museum and farm 1 hour before closing time.) www.bedesworld.co.uk

Wallsend

Segedunum Roman Fort - Bathhouse and Museum. Telephone 0191 236 9347. Two minutes' walk from Wallsend Metro. At the beginning/end of route. Passport stamping point. Admission charge, 10% reduction for English Heritage members. Family Ticket available. Open daily, April - Oct 10.00 to 17.00. Nov - March 10.00 to 15.00. (Also café and permissive water tap, ask for permission at reception desk - see relevant lists). www.twmuseums.org.uk

Gateshead

Baltic Centre for Contemporary Art. Telephone 0191 478 1810. On the Gateshead side of the Gateshead Millennium Bridge. Free admission. Open: Monday-Sunday 10.00 to 18.00. Also café and restaurant. www.balticmill.com

Newcastle

Bessie Surtees House. Telephone 0191 269 1200. Free admission. 50 metres from Trail near the Swing Bridge. Open: Mon to Fri, 10.00 to 16.00 except Bank Holidays. www.english-heritage.org.uk

Castle Keep, Castle Garth. Telephone 0191 232 7938.

Newcastle's Norman Keep, five minutes' walk from the Tyne bridge. Open: April-Sept 09.30 to 17.30. Oct-March 09.30 to 16.30. www.castlekeep-newcastle.org.uk

Museum of Antiquities. Telephone 0191 222 7849. Located in the University of Newcastle campus, nearest Metro station Haymarket. Free. Open: Mon to Sat 10.00 to 17.00. Sun closed. www.ncl.ac.uk/antiquities

Newburn

Tyne Riverside Country Park. Visitor centre. Free. Telephone 0191 264 8501. 100 metres from Trail, visible from the boat launching slipway. Visitor centre is usually open on Sat & Sun 13.00 to 17.00. Open other times depending on availability of staff. WC and water tap.

Wylam

George Stephenson's Birthplace Cottage. Telephone 01661 853457. Admission charge, National Trust members free. Grid Ref NZ 126 650. Approx 0.5 mile (0.8 km) west of Trail. Open: 17th March to 28th October 2007 and Bank Holidays, Thurs - Sun, 12.00 to 17.00. The newly refurbished tea room is also open 12.00 to 17.00 and serves meals. www.nationaltrust.org.uk

Corbridge

Corbridge Roman Site. Telephone 01434 632349. Admission charge, English Heritage members free. Signed from the town centre. Open: April - Sept 10.00 to 17.30.

Oct 10.00 to 16.00. Nov - March, weekends only 10.00 to 16.00. www.english-heritage.org.uk

Aydon Castle. Telephone 01434 632450. Admission charge, English Heritage members free. Grid Ref NZ 002 663. One mile (1.6 km) north east of Corbridge. Open: April - Sept 10.00 to 17.00. www.english-heritage.org.uk

Chollerford

Chesters Roman Fort. Telephone 01434 681379. Passport stamping point. Admission charge, English Heritage members free. On Trail. Open: April - Sept 09.30 to 18.00. Oct to March 10.00 to 16.00. Also water tap, permissive WC, café. (See relevant lists).
www.english-heritage.org.uk

Chesters Walled Garden. Telephone 01434 681483. Open: 20th March - 31st October 10.00 to 17.00. West of Chesters Fort, 0.3 km from Trail. Free admission to shop and nursery. Admission charge to garden. Unique herb garden including Roman garden. Northumberland National Park Information Point. www.chesterswalledgarden.fsnt.co.uk.

Housesteads

Housesteads Roman Fort. Telephone 01434 344363. Admission charge, English Heritage and National Trust members free. On Trail. Open: April - Sept 10.00 to 18.00. Oct - March 10.00 to 16.00. Also refreshment kiosk and watering point 0.5 mile (0.8 km) away at car park - see relevant lists). www.english-heritage.org.uk

Once Brewed

Once Brewed Visitor Centre. Telephone 01434 344396. Free. Grid Ref NY752 669. 0.5 mile (0.8 km) from Trail (accessed at Steel Rigg car park). Also WC, drinks vending machine and water tap. (See relevant lists). Internet facility. Open: Easter - 31st October 09.30 to 17.00. Winter open weekends only.

Vindolanda Roman Fort. Telephone 01434 344277. Admission charge. Grid Ref NY770664. Open: April - Sept 10.00 to 18.00. Oct - Nov 10.00 to 17.00. Last admission 45 minutes before closing time. www.vindolanda.com

Walltown

Carvoran Roman Army Museum. Telephone 016977 47485. Admission charge. 2 minutes' walk from route, from Trail turn left out of Walltown car park. Open: April - Sept 10.00 to 18.00. Oct to mid Nov 10.00 to 17.00. Last admission 30 minutes before closing time. Café for museum customers only. www.vindolanda.com

Cumbria

Gilsland

Birdoswald Roman Fort. Telephone 016977 47602. Admission charge. English Heritage members free Grid

Ref NY615 663. On Trail. Open: 1 April - 31 October 10.00 to 17.00. Café open: 10.00 to 17.00. Also passport stamping point. www.english-heritage.org.uk

Lanercost

Lanercost Priory. Telephone 016977 3030. Admission charge, English Heritage members free. Grid Ref NY556 637. 1 mile (1.6 km) from Trail. Open: April - Sept 10.00 to 17.00. Oct 10.00 to 16.00 Thurs to Mon (closed Tues and Wed). Closed Nov - March.
www.english-heritage.org.uk

Lanercost Priory Parish Church (part of priory). Donations. Open all year 09.00 to dusk.

Carlisle

Tullie House Museum. Telephone 01228 534781. Admission charge. Five minutes' walk from Trail. Open: April - June & Sept - Oct, Mon - Sat 10.00 to 17.00; Sun 12.00 to 17.00. July & Aug hours as above except Sun 11.00 to 17.00. Nov - March, Mon - Sat 10.00 to 16.00; Sun 12.00 to 16.00. No admission charge for restaurant or WC. Also café. www.tulliehouse.co.uk

Carlisle Castle. Telephone 01228 591 922. Admission charge, English Heritage members free. Free admission to shop in entrance. Five minutes' from Trail. Open: April - Sept 09.30 to 17.00. Oct - March 10.00 to 16.00. Military museum, also Roman finds exhibition in castle.

Youth hostels

There are three permanent plus two seasonal youth hostels handy for the National Trail. The following list is for guidance only, for full details refer to the YHA accommodation guide. www.yha.org.uk

Tyneside and Northumberland

Newcastle upon Tyne: 107 Jesmond Road Newcastle upon Tyne, Wear, NE2 1NJ. Email newcastle@yha.org.uk Tel: 0870 770 8868. Fax: 0191 281 8779. Internet facility. Grid Ref NZ 257 656. Nearest Metro station: Jesmond. Open all year.

Once Brewed: Military Road, Bardon Mill, Northumberland, NE47 7AN. Tel: 0870 770 8868. Email oncebrewed@yha.org.uk Fax: 01434 344045. Internet facility. Grid Ref NY752 668. Available all year by advance booking.

Greenhead: Greenhead, Brampton, Cumbria, CA8 7HG. Email dougsandragreenh@btconnect.com Tel: 01697 747411. Grid Ref NY659 655.

Cumbria

Birdoswald (seasonal): Located within Birdoswald Roman Fort, Gilsland. Open 14 July to 15 September. Email; birdoswald@yha.org.uk. Tel: 0870 770 8868. Grid Ref NY615 663.

Carlisle (seasonal): Old Brewery Residences, Bridge Lane, Caldewgate, Carlisle, Cumbria. CA2 5SR. Open 9th July to 3rd September 2007. Tel: 0870 770 5752 Email deec@impacthousing.org.uk Fax: 01228 594631. Grid Ref NY394 560.

Camping sites, barns, bunkhouses and private hostels

We strongly recommend that you obtain a copy of the Hadrian's Wall Country Mini Guide (see page 23) which contains full details of the amenities and services available at the camping sites listed in the guide. However, not all of the sites on or close to the Trail are in this year's guide so, as a service to you the walker, we have decided to list here every inspected site, plus those other non-inspected places which sometimes take in campers. For these non-accredited sites no claim can be made as to their quality standards. We do advise that you book in advance because some of the sites listed are only quite small.

Northumberland

Heddon-on-the-Wall

Houghton North Farm Visitors' Accommodation (hostel). Telephone: 01661 853370. Grid Ref NZ 125 668. Distance from Trail 0.5 mile (0.8 km). Four star. Open all year.

Harlow Hill

Well House Farm Camping & Caravanning. Contact: Kenneth Richardson. Email info@wellhousefarm.co.uk Telephone: 01661 842193. Grid Ref NZ 043 666. Distance from Trail: 1 mile (1.6 km). Open: Mar - Oct. www.wellhousefarm.co.uk

Wall

Wall village green. One night's free camping courtesy of Wall parish council. Public WC on site. No other facilities. Distance from Trail: 0.2 miles (0.4 km). Grid Ref NY928 693. Non-accredited site.

Acomb

Fallowfield Dene Caravan & Camping. Contact: Dennis and Jenny Burnell. Telephone: 01434 603553. Four star site. Distance from Trail: 2 miles (3.2 km). Grid Ref NY938 676. Open: 16th March to last Sunday in October. www.fallowfielddene.co.uk

Chollerford

Riverside camping site. Telephone 01434 681325. Contact (after 6pm 01434 681586). Contact Pauline Jewitt. Next door to the Riverside Tea Rooms. Accredited site. Open Mar - Nov.

Walwick

Green Carts Farm Camp Site & Bunkhouse. Telephone 01434 681320. Contact Sandra Maughan. Secure cycle racks and shed. Grid Ref NY887 717. Inspected site. 0.5 km from Trail. Open all year.

Barrasford

Barrasford Arms Camping Barn. Telephone 01434 681237 or YHA booking line 0870 770 8868. Email contact@barrasfordarms.co.uk Distance from Trail: 2.5 miles (4.2 km). Open all year. www.barrasfordarms.co.uk

Northumberland National Park

Old Repeater Station (hostel). Telephone 01434 688668 or 07941 238641. Grid Ref NY816 701. 0.5 mile (0.8 km) from the Trail. Dormitory accommodation. Secure cycle racks and shed. Open all year.

Gibbs Hill Farm (Bunkhouse). Telephone: 01434 344030. Contact: Valerie Gibson. Distance from Trail 1.5 miles. Grid Ref NY749691. Open all year. www.gibbshillfarm.co.uk.

Winshields Farm Camping. Telephone: 01434 344243. Distance from Trail 0.5 miles (0.8 km). Grid Ref NY745 669. Open: 1 April - 31 October. www.winshields.co.uk

Hadrian's Wall Caravan and Camping Site. Contact: Graham Reed. Telephone 01434 320495. Three star site. Distance from Trail: 0.6 mile (1.0 km). Grid Ref NY730 658. Pick-up and drop-off service by prior arrangement. Open all year except February.

Holmhead (camping barn). Telephone 016977 47402. Grid Ref NY662 660. On the Trail. Open except Christmas and New Year. www.bandbhadrianswall.com

Greenhead

Roam 'n' Rest Caravan Park (camping). Contact: Joan Waugh. Telephone 016977 47213. Three star site. Grid Ref NY655 654. Distance from Trail 0.5 miles (0.8 km).

Open: March - Oct. Weather dependant. Please check with owner.

Cumbria

Banks

Banks Head Camping Barn. For information telephone 016977 3198; for bookings telephone YHA booking line 0870 770 8868. On the Trail. Grid Ref NY579 649. Open: all year.

Walton

Centurion Inn. Non accredited campsite Telephone 016977 2438 for details.

Sandysike Bunkhouse & Camping site. Telephone 016977 2330. Pending inspection. On the Trail Email sandysike@talk21.com

Laversdale

Stonewall Farm Campsite. Telephone 01228 573666. Non-accredited camping site, please telephone for details. Grid Ref: NY477624.

Crosby

Bluebell Camping Barn. Contact Joanne Harper. Telephone: 01228 573600. Grid Ref NY455596. Just off the Trail. Opens July 2007, will then be open all year. Email joanneharper1@aol.com

Houghton
Green Acres Caravan Park (camping). Telephone 01228 675418. Grid Ref NY418 615. Distance from Trail 2.5 miles. Open: 1 April - 31 Oct.

Black Ford
Dandy Dinmont Caravan Park (camping). Contact Barbara Inglis. Telephone 01228 674611. Four star site. Grid Ref NY396 619. Distance from Trail 3.5 miles. On A7 bus route from Carlisle. Open: 1 March - 31 Oct.

Grinsdale
West View Camping and Caravan site. Open April to October. Email jandcedgar@aol.com Telephone 01228 526336. Contact John Edgar. Distance from Trail 0.5 miles. Grid Ref NY365 572.

Boustead Hill
Hillside Farm Bunk Barn. Telephone 01228 576398. Contact Sandra Rudd. Five minutes' walk from Trail. Grid Ref NY293591. Open all year but check with owner in winter.

Port Carlisle
Chapel Side Campsite and Camping Barn. Kirkland House Farm. Telephone 016973 51400. Contact Daphne Hogg. Camping barn to open Summer 07. Five minutes' walk

from Trail. Open all year but check with owner in winter. Non-accredited site.

Bowness-on-Solway

Bowness village hall. Telephone 016973 51322. By arrangement, groups can book the hall for basic sleeping accommodation. You will need to supply your own sleeping bags and camping mats as no mattresses are available.

The Old Chapel. Telephone: 016973 51126. Contact: Maureen Miller. Grid Ref: NY224627. On the trail. Group accommodation available by prior agreement. Please check with owner. Also car parking, shop and café available (See relevant lists). www.oldchapelbownessonsolway.com

Obtaining cash & paying for things

On several occasions in the past B&B owners have ended up driving walkers to the nearest cash-point machine because their guests were ill-prepared for the fact that, apart from the larger hotels, very few small businesses accept payments by debit or credit cards. With just a little planning this needn't happen. Together, the available cash-point machines and Post Offices (where you can draw out cash if you bank with Alliance and Leicester, Bank of Ireland, Barclays, Clydesdale Bank, Co-op, Nationwide, Lloyds TSB or Smile) offer ample places to obtain money. Pay particular attention to the opening times of the small Post Offices.

Shops

A handful of shops (refer list of shops) also allow payment by debit/credit card and some also have the cash-back facility. (See the list of shops for details). To pay by using this method your card must have the MAESTRO symbol on it.

Cashing travellers' cheques

This will be of interest to our guests from overseas. Banks will, of course, cash travellers' cheques, but you can also cash them at the main post offices in Carlisle and Newcastle. The small post offices will not cash travellers' cheques.

Using cash-point machines if you are from overseas

You may use your bank ATM card in most UK bank cash-point machines if your card has the CIRRUS symbol on it.

Bureau de Change

There is a Bureau de Change in the Royal Quays ferry terminal that is open for the arrival of ferries from Holland and Scandinavia. The main banks in Newcastle will also exchange foreign currency.

Cash-point machines

This list is necessarily selective, it includes those cash-point machines that we think will be most useful to you. Some are in the towns and villages close by where walkers typically find B&Bs. (We do welcome suggestions for machines that you think should be in next year's guide). Bank opening hours are also shown. All banks have a cash-point machine unless otherwise stated.

Tyneside and Northumberland

Wallsend

The following cash-point machines and banks are in High Street West. Five minutes' walk from Segedunum; from the site walk up Station Road to the traffic lights. Turn left for:

Lloyds TSB. Open: Mon, Tues, Fri 09.30 to 16.30. Wed from 10.00.

Barclays. Open: Mon - Fri 09.00 to 17.00; Sat 09.00 to 13.00.

Northern Rock. cash-point machine

Turn right for:

Halifax & Nationwide. cash-point machines.

Lloyds TSB (yes, another!). Open: Mon - Fri 09.00 to 17.00; Sat 09.00 to 13.00.

Newcastle

Central station has three cash-point machines located next to the confectionery shop, approaching platform 2. The machines belong to Nat West; Abbey National and Royal Bank of Scotland. To obtain money while walking the Trail in Newcastle we suggest that, using the Tyne Bridge as a landmark, you walk up Dean Street which leads into Grey Street where you will find banks and cash-point machines very close to each other and in the following order:

Royal Bank of Scotland. Open: Mon - Fri 09.15 to 16.45. (Opens 09.45 on Wed).

Bank of Scotland. Open: Mon - Fri 09.15 to 16.45. (Opens 09.45 on Wed).

Barclays. Pilgrim Street: (just off Grey Street). Open: Mon - Fri 09.00 to 16.30, Sat 09.00 - 12.00.

Lloyds TSB. Open: Mon - Fri 09.00 to 17.00 (Opens 10.00 on Tues), Sat 9.30 to 12.30.

Nat West. Open: Mon - Fri 09.00 to 17.00. (Opens 9.30 on Wed).

HSBC (beside Grey's Monument). Open: Mon, Tues, Wed, Fri 09.00 to 17.00. Thurs 09.00 to 19.00. Sat 09.00 to 17.00. (It is only 10 minutes' walk from the Tyne bridge to Grey's monument, the centre of Newcastle's shopping district).

Newburn

Lloyds TSB, Station Road. Open: Mon - Fri 09.30 to 16.30. (Opens 10.00 on Thursday).

Barclays, Station Road. No cash-point machine, open: Mon - Fri 10.00 to 16.00.

Heddon-on-the-Wall

Spar Supermarket and Shell garage. Telephone 01661 852276. Open: Mon - Sat 07.00 to 21.00; Sun 08.00 to 21.00. Cash-point machine inside shop (UK banks only) for which a charge is made; permissive WC & water tap outside (see relevant lists).

Corbridge

Barclays. Market Place. Open: Mon - Fri 09.30 to 16.00.

Hexham

HSBC. Fore Street. Open: Mon - Fri 09.30 to 16.30.

Barclays. Priestpopple. Open: Mon, Wed, Thur 13.30 to 15.00. Tues, Fri 11.00 to 15.00.

Lloyds TSB. Priestpopple. Open: Mon - Fri 09.00 to 17.00 (Closes 16.00 on Wed), Sat 09.30 to 12.30.

Nat West Battle Hill. Open: Mon - Fri 09.00 to 16.30. (Opens 9.30 on Wed).

Haltwhistle

HSBC. Market square. Open: Mon - Fri 09.30 to 16.30.

Barclays Westgate. Open: Mon - Fri 09.30 to 16.30. (Opens 10.00 Wed).

Cumbria

Gilsland

Post office and General store. Free cash point in store. Shop open: Mon - Wed 07.30 to 12.30 & 13.30 to 17.30. Thurs 07.30 to 12.30. Fri 07.30 to 12.30 & 13.30 to 17.30. Sat 07.30 to 12.30.

Brampton

HSBC. Front Street. Open: Mon - Fri 09.30 to 16.30.

Barclays. Front Street. Open: Mon - Fri 09.30 to 16.30.

Carlisle

HSBC. English Street. Open: Mon - Fri 09.00 to 17.00, Sat 09.00 to 17.00.

Barclays. English Street. Open: Mon - Sat 09.00 to 17.00. Sat 09.00 to 15.30.

Clydesdale. English Street. Open: Mon - Fri 09.15 to 16.45. (Opens 09.45 on Wed). Sat 09.00 to 13.00.

Nat West. English Street. Open: Mon - Fri 09.00 to 16.30. (Opens 09.30 on Wed). Sat 09.30 to 13.30.

Northern Rock. Devonshire Street. Open: Mon - Fri 09.00 to 17.00. (Opens 09.30 Tues). Sat 09.00 to 12.00. 0.5 (0.8km) mile east of Port Carlisle

Glendale Caravan Park. Telephone 016973 51317. Cash-point machine on site from May 07 for which a small charge is made. Also site shop and bar meals open to walkers. (see page 81).

Water taps

Finding somewhere to fill your water bottles on a hot sunny day can, if you are unlucky, occupy your mind to the point of distraction. We have done our best to prepare a list of places where you can replenish your supplies without recourse to knocking on doors, which in any case is not encouraged.

There is now a string of water taps that we will hopefully continue to add to over time, as well as other places, granted on a permissive basis, where owners have kindly agreed to let you call for water. Please respect the goodwill that many folk have shown. Three churches have offered the use of their outdoor water taps - please consider leaving them a small donation in appreciation.

For all sites the taps are advertised as a summer only amenity.

Tyneside and Northumberland

Segedunum Roman Fort. See opening times in list of historic sites, museums and visitor centres. Permissive water tap, ask at the reception desk. (Also café, WCs, see other lists).

St Peter's Marina Office (Indoor tap): Telephone: 0191 265 4472. Available daily, 24 hours. Location: St Peter's Basin, east side of bascule bridge, on the Trail). Please note that this is a permissive water tap, courtesy of the Marina owners.

St Margaret's Church. Denton Road, on the Trail. Available Mon - Fri 09.00 to 17.00. There is also a café here open Tuesday and Thursday 10.30 to 14.30.

Newburn Sports Centre. Five minutes' walk from the Trail at Newburn. From the boat launching slipway walk towards the visitor centre, turn right, pass the Keelman Inn, the sports centre is a tall modern brick building about 100 metres past the Keelman. Open: Mon - Fri 09.00 to 22.00. Sat & Sun: 09.00 to 17.00. WC, ask at the reception desk. Cold drinks and confectionary vending machines. Walkers can pay to use the showers.

Newburn. Tyne Riverside Country Park Visitor Centre. Visible from the boat launching slipway. Water available from the WC which is open daily 09.00 to 17.00.

Heddon-on-the-Wall, Spar supermarket & Shell garage. Permissive water tap. (Also WC, general store, cash machine, see relevant lists).

Whittledene reservoirs. 0.6 mile (1 km) west of Harlow Hill, to the south of the B6318. Situated at Grid Ref NZ 065 680 at the reservoir site, part of the fishing club. Permissive tap, also WC, courtesy of Northumbrian Water.

Chesters Roman Fort, Chollerford. Signed from the B6318, the Trail passes the site entrance. Request permission in shop. (Also WC, café, see relevant lists). See site opening times in list of historic sites, museums and visitor centres.

Housesteads Roman Fort. Located in the car park close to the shop entrance. It is approx 0.5 mile (0.8 km) from the Trail at the bottom of the hill. Available any time. (Also WC, refreshments, see WC and café lists).

Once Brewed Visitor Centre. Approx 0.5 mile (0.8 km) from the Trail, leave the route at Steel Rigg car park. Located in the Visitor Centre car park near the pay and display ticket machine. Available any time. Also WC, Internet facility and drinks vending machine (see lists).

Cawfields Quarry car park. On the Trail. Located on the toilet block wall, available any time.

Greenhead Hotel. Grid Ref NY660 654. 0.5 km south of the Trail in Greenhead village. The owners have very kindly agreed to allow walkers to use the water supply in the hotel during the summer season. It will be available during the day.

Cumbria

Heads Wood. Grid Ref NY503 632. Permissive water tap. Located inside westerley garden fence on gate post.

Crosby Lodge Hotel. External permissive water tap at hotel, through gateway from Trail. (Also refreshments for walkers, and restaurant, see other lists).

Sands Sports Centre, Carlisle. On the Trail, also a passport stamping station. Permissive water tap, ask at reception. Available normal opening hours, see page 73. (Also café, WC, see other lists).

Beaumont - St Mary's Churchyard. On the Trail. Walk clockwise around the church to find the tap in a wooden cupboard. Permissive water tap.

Drumburgh, The Grange farm. Telephone 01228 576551. Permissive water tap and disabled WC, also drinks vending machine (see relevant lists). Located up cul-de-sac opposite junction in village, from where it will be signed. Open: 08.00 to 18.00 until end of September, other times by arrangement.

Port Carlisle, Solway Methodist Church. Telephone 01228 576551. Grid Ref NY242619. On the Trail. A quiet place for retreat. Permissive WC and water tap available. Open: Easter - September from morning to early evening.

Bowness-on-Solway. Located in St Michael's Churchyard, two minutes' walk from the Trail. Walk clockwise around the church to find the permissive water tap.

WCs

Tyneside and Northumberland

Segedunum Roman Fort. Telephone 0191 295 5757. Two minutes' walk from Wallsend Metro. Permissive WC (and water tap), ask at reception desk. Also Passport stamping point. See list of historic sites for opening etc. times.

St Peter's Marina Office. Telephone: 0191 265 4472. Available Mon - Sun 09.00 to 17.00. (Location: St Peter's Basin, east side of bascule bridge over marina entrance, on the Trail). Permissive WC, call at office.

Newcastle Quayside. East end of Swing Bridge, public WC, 20p coin in slot.

Newburn. Tyne Riverside Country Park Visitor Centre. One minute's walk from the boat launching slipway. Water is also available from the WC which is open daily 09.00 to 17.00.

Newburn Sports Centre. Five minutes' walk from the Trail at Newburn. From the boat launching slipway walk towards the Visitor Centre, turn right towards the Keelman Inn. The sports centre is a tall modern brick building about 150 metres from the Keelman. Open: Mon - Fri 09.00 to 22.00; Sat & Sun 09.00 to 17.00. Also permissive water tap, ask at the reception desk. Cold drinks and confectionary vending machines. Walkers can pay to use the showers.

Heddon-on-the-Wall, Spar supermarket & Shell garage. Permissive WC. (Also water tap, general store, cash machine (see relevant lists).

Whittledene reservoirs. 0.6 mile (1 km) west of Harlow Hill, to the south of the B6318. Situated at Grid Ref 065 680 at the reservoir site, part of the fishing club facilities. Permissive water tap and WC, both amenities courtesy of Northumbrian Water.

Chesters Roman Fort, Chollerford. Signed from the B6318, the Trail passes in front of site entrance. Permissive WC, ask at reception desk before use. English Heritage have agreed to let genuine Trail walkers use the site WC - but please consider purchasing something from the shop if you are not visiting the site. (Note free admission to English Heritage members). (Also, café on site, see relevant lists for opening etc. times).

Housesteads Roman Fort. Located in the car park close to the shop entrance, approx 0.5 mile (0.8 km) from the Trail at the bottom of the hill. Closed at night. Also refreshments, see list of cafés.

Once Brewed Visitor Centre. Approx 0.5 mile (0.8 km) from the Trail, leave the route at Steel Rigg car park. Also water tap and drinks vending machine (see relevant lists).

Cawfields Quarry car park. On the Trail route, available any time. (Also water tap - see relevant list for details).

Walltown Quarry car park. On the Trail route, available any time.

Greenhead Hotel. Grid Ref NY660 654. 0.5 km south of the Trail in Greenhead village. The owners have very kindly agreed to allow walkers to use the WC in the hotel. It will be available during the day.

Cumbria

Gilsland. Public WC, five minutes' walk from the Trail route. At the village school car park walk into the main street, the WC is signed, approximately 30 metres up-hill from the shop/Post Office.

Sands Sports Centre. Telephone 01228 625222. On the Trail. WC in reception area. Open: 09.00 to 21.30 daily.

Drumburgh, the Grange farm. Telephone 01228 576551. Permissive disabled WC, also drinks vending machine, and permissive water tap (see relevant lists). On the Trail, located up cul-de-sac opposite junction in village, from where it will be signed. Open: 08.00 to 18.00 until the end of September, other times by arrangement.

Port Carlisle, Solway Methodist Church. Telephone 01228 576551. Grid Ref NY242619. A quiet place for retreat. Permissive water tap and WC available. Open: Easter - Sept from morning to early evening.

Bowness-on-Solway. WC available in the village hall. Next to the King's Arms. Open daily in daylight hours from approx 09.00 to 22.00. Closed 4pm in winter.

Shops and Post Offices

When you sit down to plan your trip do make a note of where all the shops are. You will, of course, find plenty of food shops in Wallsend, Newcastle and Carlisle and it is not practicable to mention them all, so this list is selective. We have tried to include every general store, Post Office and anything else that we think you need to know about either on the Trail itself, or within easy reach of it. Some walkers' tips are included. Where the larger settlements have a wider range of shops this is indicated. Many of the shops are also Post Offices. They are particularly useful if you bank with Alliance and Leicester, Bank of Ireland, Barclays, Clydesdale Bank, Co-op, Nationwide, Lloyds TSB or Smile because you can also **draw out cash from them**. You will need your ATM card and your pin number. The Post Office hours are not necessarily the same as the shop opening hours so please take note. Note that every Post Office now sells **electronic mobile phone top-ups.** (See also the separate section on obtaining money).

Tyneside and Northumberland

Wallsend

Nearest Metro station is Wallsend. Contains a wide range of general shops and supermarkets. Because you might be stocking up on provisions here the supermarket nearest to Segedunum is mentioned below.

Co-op. The Forum shopping centre. Five minutes' walk from Segedunum, from the site walk up Station Road to the traffic lights, the Forum is across the road to your left. Open: Mon - Sat 08.00 to 20.00. Sun 10.00 to 16.00. Cashback & mobile phone top-ups.

Post Office. Located inside the Co-op. Telephone: 0191 263 0642. Open: Mon-Fri 0800 to 1730. Sat 09.00 to 15.00.

Newcastle city centre

Contains the usual city centre range of shops, supermarkets, restaurants etc. The nearest supermarket to the Trail is Tesco Express in Broad Chare, off the Quayside (open daily 06.00 to 23.00).

Post Office. Located inside Eldon Square shopping centre. Open: Mon - Sat 09.00 to 17.30.

Newcastle Business Park

Riverside Newsagent. Telephone 0191 226 0686. Open: Mon - Fri 07.00 to 16.30. Located only 30 metres from the route, across the adjacent road, a short distance west of Dunston Staithes (large pier structure in the River Tyne). You will also find a café bar and deli. (See page 83).

Newburn

(No general shops apart from a fish and chip shop and newsagent).

Post Office. Station Road. Telephone 0191 267 4241.

Open: Mon & Tue 08.30 to 17.30. Wed 08.00 to 17.00. Thurs & Fri 08.30 to 17.30. Sat 08.30 to 12.30.

Heddon-on-the-Wall

Post Office and newsagent. Telephone: 01661 853433.

Shop open: Mon - Sat: 07.15 to 18.00; Sun: 07.15 to 12.00.

Post office open: Mon - Fri 09.00 to 17.30; Sat 09.00 to 12.30.

Dingle Dell Delicatessen (and tea room). Telephone: 01661 854 325. Open: Summer Mon - Fri 09.00 to 17.30, Sat 09.30 to 17.00. Winter Mon - Fri 09.00 to 17.00, Sat 09.30 to 17.00. Packed lunches also available.

Spar Supermarket and Shell garage. Telephone 01661 852276. Open: Mon - Sat 07.00 to 21.00; Sun 08.00 to 21.00. Also cash machine inside shop (UK banks only) for which a charge is made; permissive WC & water tap (see relevant lists). Mobile phone electronic top-ups.

Wylam

Spar supermarket. Telephone 01661 852214. Open Sun - Sat: 06.00 to 21.00. Cashback facility & mobile phone top-ups.

Post Office. Telephone 01661 852241. Open Mon - Tues: 09.00 to 12.30pm & 13.30 to 17.30. Wed 09.00

to 12.30. Thurs - Fri: 09.00 to 12.30 & 13.30 to 17.30. Sat: 09.00 to 12.30.

Delicatessen and Tea Shop. Telephone 01661 852552. Shop open Mon - Sat: 07.30 to 17.30. Tea room open: Mon - Sat: 08.00 to 16.00.

B6318 Military Road

Vallum Farm Tearoom & Farm shop. Telephone: 01434 672652. Tearooms open 10.00 to 16.30 daily. Farm shop open 10.00 to 18.00 daily. Grid Ref NZ049683. A short walk from the Trail situated on the south side of the B6318.

Corbridge

Contains a small range of general shops.

Co-op, Hill Street. Telephone 01434 632007. Open: Mon - Sat 07.00 to 22.00. Sun 08.00 to 22.00. Cashback facility.

Post Office and newsagent. Town Hall Buildings. Newsagent open: Mon - Fri 05.00 to 17.30. Sat 05.00 to 18.00. Sun 05.00 to 12.30.

Post Office open: Mon - Fri 08.30 to 17.30. Sat 08.30 to 12.30. Telephone: 01434 632042.

Acomb

Post Office and Shop. Telephone 01434 603743. Open: Mon, Tues, Thurs, Fri: 09.00 to 17.30 (closed for lunch 12.30 to 13.30). Wed: 09.00 to 13.00. Sat: 09.00 to 12.30.

Hexham

Contains a wide range of supermarkets and general shops, restaurants etc.

Post Office. Fore Street. Located within department store. Telephone 01434 602001. Post Office open: Mon - Tues 08.30 to 17.30; Wed 09.00 to 17.30; Thurs 08.30 to 17.30; Fri 08.30 to 17.30; Sat 08.30 to 16.00.

Humshaugh

~~Post Office and~~ **general store.** Telephone 01434 681258. ~~Post office open: Mon 09.00 to 12.00 & 13.00 to 17.00. Tues to Fri 09.00 to 13.00. Sat 09.00 to 12.00~~.

Shop open: Mon 07.30 to 17.00. Tues to Fri 07.30 to 13.00. Sat 07.30 to 12.00. Sun 09.00 to 12.00.

Haydon Bridge

Co-op and Post Office. Telephone 01434 684327. Shop & Post Office open: Sun 09.00 to 22.00; Mon & Tues 08.00 to 22.00; Wed 08.00 to 22.00 (post office to 21.00); Thurs - Sat 08.00 to 22.00. Electronic mobile phone top-ups.

Haltwhistle

Contains a wide range of general shops.

Post Office. Main Street. Telephone 01434 320361. Open: Mon - Tues 09.00 to 12.30 & 13.30 to 17.30. Wed 09.00 to 12.30. Thur - Fri 09.00 to 12.30 & 13.30 to 17.30. Sat 09.00 to 12.30.

Co-op supermarket. Main Street. Telephone 01434 321188. Open: Mon - Sat 08.00 to 22.00. Sun 10.00 to 16.00. Cashback facility.

United Co-op supermarket. Telephone 01434 320392. Open: Mon - Sat: 08.00 to 22.00. Sun: 10.00 to 16.00. Cashback facility.

Cumbria

Gilsland

Post Office and general store. Telephone 016977 47211. Post office open: Mon - Wed 09.00 to 12.30 & 13.30 to 17.30. Thurs 09.00 to 12.30. Fri 09.00 to 12.30 & 13.30 to 17.30. Sat 09.00 to 12.30.

Shop open: Mon - Wed 07.30 to 12.30 & 13.30 to 17.30. Thurs 07.30 to 12.30. Fri 07.30 to 12.30 & 13.30 to 17.30. Sat 07.30 to 12.30. Free cash point in store available when shop open.

Brampton

Contains a wide range of general shops.

Brampton Post Office. 5 Front Street. Telephone 016977 2301. Bureau de change. Open: Mon - Fri 09.00 to 17.30. Sat 09.00 to 12.30.

Walton

Centurion Inn. Post Office in pub. 016977 2438. Open: Mon and Wed 09.30 to 12.00.

Irthington

Post Office and shop. Telephone 016977 2300. Contact Diane Davidson. Post office opening times normally same as shop: Mon - Fri 08.45 to 12.30 & 13.00 to 18.30; Sat 08.45 to 13.00; Sun 09.30 to 12.30.

Carlisle

Expect to find an extensive range of shops in this bustling city centre.

Main Post Office. Warwick Road (Near Railway Station). Bureau de change. Open: Mon - Fri 08.30 to 17.30. Sat 09.00 to 17.30.

Post Office and Shop, Scotch Street. Telephone 01228 525017. Open: Mon - Fri 09.00 to 17.30. Sat 09.00 to 17.00.

Burgh-by-Sands

Post Office and shop. Telephone 01228 576342. Open: Mon & Thurs 09.00 to 12.00 & 15.00 to 17.00.

Drumburgh

The Grange Farm, 'Laal Bite'. Telephone 01228 576551. Drinks vending machine, also permissive water tap and disabled WC. Located up cul-de-sac opposite junction in village, from where it will be signed. Open: 08.00 to 18.00, until end of September, other times by arrangement. 0.5 (0.8 km) mile east of Port Carlisle.

Glendale Caravan Park. Telephone 016973 51317. Site general shop open to walkers plus bar meals. Cashpoint machine for which a small charge is made. Grid Ref NY244612.

Bowness-on-Solway

Post Office. Cold refreshments. Open: Mon, Wed & Thur 09.00 to 15.00. Closed for lunch 12.00 to 13.00.

The Old Chapel. Telephone: 016973 51126. Contact: Maureen Miller. Grid Ref: NY224627. On the Trail. Light refreshments and local produce available 10.00 to 16.00 every day except Tuesday. Packed lunches available with prior arrangement. Full disabled facilities. Also car parking and group accommodation available. Please check with owner. www.oldchapelbownessonsolway.com

Cafés *(and other places where you will find refreshments)*

This list excludes pubs and restaurants. There are several cafés on or close to the Trail as well as other places that offer some form of refreshment that we have decided to include in this list. Note their opening times and arrangements.

Tyneside and Northumberland

Wallsend

Cafés and places to eat are numerous in High Street and in the Forum shopping centre. As a general rule the cafés are shut all day Sunday.

Segedunum Roman Fort. Café available during opening hours. See list of historic sites, museums and visitor centres for full details of site.

Newcastle Quayside

Millennium Bridge, Baltic Centre and Sage Music Centre area of Quayside. Numerous cafés and bars and also sandwich and hot drink barrows during the day.

Gateshead

Baltic Centre for Contemporary Art. Telephone 0191 478 1810. On the Gateshead side of the Gateshead Millennium Bridge. Free admission. Open: Mon - Sun 10.00 to 18.00. Café open gallery hours (Food served until 17.30). Restaurant open 12.00 to 1400 & 19.00 to 21.45 (Closed Sunday evenings).

Newcastle Business Park

You will find the following premises approx 30 metres across the road, adjacent to the Trail, a short way to the west of Dunston Staithes (a large pier structure in the river Tyne).

The Deli. Telephone 0191 272 0544. Open: Mon - Fri 07.00 to 15.00.

Lemington

Lemington Community Centre. Telephone 0191 264 1959. 25 metres from the Trail, look out for sandwich board. Open: Mon - Fri 09.00 to 16.00. Grid Ref: NZ183647. Internet facility. www.lemingtoncentre.co.uk.

Wylam Waggonway

Stephenson's birthplace cottage. Telephone 01661 853457. This National Trust site, situated on the Wylam Waggonway, is approx 0.5 mile (0.8 km) west of the Trail at Grid Ref NZ 126 650, and less than a mile (approx 1 km) from Wylam (shop; café; pharmacy; pubs) where many walkers find accommodation. It is the birthplace of George Stephenson and so, quite literally therefore, the cradle of the railway age. Besides the interest in the site itself (it is also haunted) a delightful small tea room that now serves meals, whose staff sometimes dress in period costume, will assure you of a warm welcome. The cottage is open from 17h March to 28 October 2007 Thurs - Sun, 12.00 to 17.00 and bank holiday Mondays. If your itinerary allows you the time, the combination of the café and historic interest makes this a top tip.

Heddon-on-the-Wall
Dingle Dell Tea Room. (Look out for a sign in the village to Heddon shopping centre). Telephone 01661 854325. Open: Mon - Fri 09.00 to 17.30. Sat 09.30 to 16.30.

Wylam
Tea Shop & Delicatessen. Telephone 01661 852552. Tea shop open: Mon - Sat 08.00 to 16.00.

B6318 Military Road
Vallum Farm Tearoom & Farm shop. Telephone: 01434 672652. Tearooms open 10.00 to 16.30 daily. Farm shop open 10.00 to 18.00 daily. Grid Ref NZ049683. To the south side of the B6318, opposite side of road to the Trail.

Corbridge
There are several cafés and eating places in Corbridge.

B6318 Military Road
St. Oswald's Café. Telephone 01434 689010. On the trail. Grid Ref: NY940 694. Open: March/April/Nov Fri, Sat, Sun 10.00 to 16.30. May - Oct daily 10.00 to 16.30. Closed Monday.

Chollerford

Riverside Tea Rooms. Telephone 01434 681325. Next to garage, on west side of roundabout. Open: Daily 09.00 to 17.00. Internet access.

Luculus Larder, Chesters Roman Fort. Telephone 01434 681781. Open: April - October 10.00 to 17.00. (N.B. For use by Chesters Fort visitors only).

B6318 Military Road, Northumberland National Park

Housesteads Roman Fort. (Joint National Trust/English Heritage). National Trust shop, info centre and refreshments kiosk. Telephone 01434 344525. Open: daily April - Oct 10.00 to 18.00; rest of year 10.00 to 16.00. (Closed Christmas/Boxing Day and New Year's Day).

Once Brewed

Once Brewed Visitor Centre. Telephone 01434 344396. Open: April - Oct 09.30 to 17.00 daily. Open weekends in winter 10.00 to 15.00. Hot drinks vending machine only. Internet access.

Walltown

Walltown Refreshments. Telephone 016977 47121. Open 10.00 daily Easter to November. Credit and debit cards accepted.

Haltwhistle

Haltwhistle itself has a good range of general shops and cafés.

Herding Hill Farm shop and coffee shop. Telephone 01434 320668. Open Tues - Thurs 10.00 to 16.00. Fri - Sat 10.00 to 17.00. Sun 10.00 to 16.30. All year and open Bank Holiday Mondays. Grid Ref: NY712649. Hot meals and sandwiches served.

Gilsland

House of Meg Tea Room. Mumps Hall, Hall Terrace. Telephone 016977 47716. Open: Mon - Fri 07.30 to 17.30. Sat 08.00 to 17.30. Sun 10.00 to 16.00.

Birdoswald Roman Fort. Telephone 016977 47602. Open: 1 April - 31 October 10.00 to 17.00 daily. Tea Room open: 10.00 to 17.00. Also permissive WC and water tap (During opening hours). Passport stamping station. www.english-heritage.org.uk

Lanercost

Haytongate. Telephone 016977 41119 (weekday office hours). Grid Ref NY554 645. From Easter to late October self-service hot and cold drinks and snacks available when notice is displayed. Hadrian's Wall T-Shirts available weekday office hours.

Brampton

Contains a wide range of general shops.

Crosby

High Crosby Farm. Telephone: 01228 573216. Self-service point. Refreshments available April - October.

Carlisle

Café at the Sands Sports Centre. Telephone 01228 625526. Open: 10.00 to 20.00 daily (Sports Centre open 09.00 to 21.30). Also permissive water tap. On the Trail, also a passport stamping station.

Tullie House Museum. Telephone 01228 534781. Five minutes' walk from the Trail, opposite the castle. Restaurant open: Mon - Sat 09.30 to 17.00. Sun 12.00 to 17.00 All year except Christmas day and New year's day. www.tulliehouse.co.uk

Drumburgh

The Grange Farm, 'Laal Bite'. Telephone 01228 576551. Drinks vending machine, also permissive water tap and disabled WC. Located up cul-de-sac, opposite junction in village. Open: 08.00 to 18.00, until 31st October, other times by arrangement.

Port Carlisle

Glendale Caravan Park. Telephone 016973 51317. Site general shop and bar meals available for walkers. Cash-point machine for which a small charge is made. Grid Ref NY244612.

Bowness-on-solway

The Old Chapel. Telephone: 016973 51126. Contact: Maureen Miller. Grid Ref NY224627. Light refreshments available daily from 10 .00 to 16.00 except Tuesdays. Pack lunches available with prior arrangement. Full disabled facilities. Shop, group accommodation and car parking also available (see relevant lists). www.oldchapelbownessonsolway.com

Pub restaurants en route

This list includes the pubs with restaurants actually on the route itself or close enough to be useful to you. Rest assured that there are many more in the surrounding towns and villages where you are likely to spend your evenings.

Tyneside and Northumberland

Newburn

The Keelmans. Telephone 0191 267 0772. Open: Mon - Sat 11.00 - 23.00; Sun 12.00 to 22.30. Food served: 12.00 to 21.00 daily. Location: Grange Road; from the boat launch slipway walk towards the Visitor Centre, turn right, the pub is two minutes walk on the left.

Wylam

There are pubs and restaurants in Wylam that serve food.

Heddon-on-the-Wall

The Swan. Telephone 01661 853161. Open: Mon - Sat 11.00 to 23.00, Sun 12.00 to 22.30. Food served: Mon - Sat 11.00 to 21.30, Sun 11.00 to 19.00.

B6318 Military Road

Robin Hood Inn. Telephone 01434 672273. Approx one mile (1.6 km) west of the Whittledene reservoirs on the B6318. Grid Ref NZ 050 684. Open: 12.00 to

15.00 & 17.00 to 23.00 daily & 10.00 to 23.00 during summer holidays. Food served: Mon - Fri 12.00 to 14.30 & 18.00 to 21.30 & 12.00 to 21.00 in the summer. Sunday lunch 12.00 to 16.00. Coffee served 10.00 to 12.00 in summer.

Errington Arms. Telephone 01434 672250. West side of the A68 roundabout. Grid Ref NY987 686. Open: 11.00 to 15.00 & 18.00 to 23.00 (Closed Sunday evening and Monday all day). Food served: 12.00 to 14.30 & 18.30 to 21.30, Sunday lunch 12.00 to 15.00.

Corbridge

Corbridge has several pubs and restaurants that serve food.

Wall village

The Hadrian. Telephone 01434 681232. Grid Ref NY916 688. Open: 11.00 to 23.00 daily. Food served: 12.00 to 20.45 daily.

Chollerford

The George Hotel. Telephone 01434 681611. Bar Open: 11.00 to 23.00 daily. Food served: 18.00 to 21.30 daily.

Hexham

There are several pubs, takeaways and restaurants in Hexham.

Once Brewed

Twice Brewed Inn. Telephone 01434 344534. Grid Ref NY752 669. Open: Mon - Sat 11.00 to 23.00. Sun 12.00 to 22.30. Food served: Sun - Thur 12.00 to 20.30. Fri - Sat 12.00 to 21.00. Walkers breakfast available: Easter - End Sept 8.00 to 9.00. No smoking restaurant. Disabled toilet. Internet facility.

B6318 Military Road

Milecastle Inn. Telephone 01434 321372. 0.5 mile (0.8 km) from Cawfields car park Milecastle 42. Grid Ref NY716 660. Open: 11.00 to 23.00 daily, April to October. Nov - April closes 15.00 to 18.00. Food served 12.00 to 15.00 & 18.00 to 21.00 Nov - April & 12.00 to 21.00 April - Oct.

Haltwhistle

Has several pubs and restaurants that serve food.

Greenhead

Greenhead Hotel. Telephone 016977 47411. Grid Ref NY660 654. Open: 12.00 to midnight daily from Easter. Food served: 12.00 to 20.30 daily. Sundays 12.00 to 15.00 & 17.30 to 20.30.

Cumbria

Gilsland

Samson Inn. Telephone 016977 47220. Open: Sun - Wed 12.00 to midnight. Thur - Sat 12.00 to 01.30. Food served: 12.00 to 15.00 & 16.00 to 21.00 daily. Non smoking.

Bridge Inn. Telephone 016977 47353. Open: Early May - late October Mon to Fri 12.00 to 23.00. Sat - Sun 12.00 to 12.30. Snacks available & non-accredited camping to rear of pub.

Station Hotel. Telephone 016977 47338. Open: Sat - Sun 12.00 to 23.00.

Walton

Centurion Inn. Telephone 016977 2438. Open: 11.00 to 23.00 daily. Bar meals served: 12.00 to 21.00 daily. Lunch menu served: 11.30 to 17.00 daily. Evening meals 18.00 to 20.45. On the Trail.

Laversdale

The Sportsman. Telephone 01228 573255. Open: Mon - Thur 17.00 to 23.00. Fri 16.00 to 23.00. Sat - Sun 12.00 to 23.00. Food Mon - Thur 18.00 to 20.30. Fri 16.00 to 21.00. Sat - Sun 12.00 to 21.00. Pub located approx one mile (1.6 km) from Grid Ref 488 618 - link signed as a bridleway.

Crosby

Stag Inn. Telephone 01228 573210. Open: 10.00 to 23.00 daily. Food 12.00 to 14.00 & 18.00 to 21.00 daily.

Carlisle

You will find a large selection of pubs and restaurants in Carlisle.

Burgh by Sands

The Greyhound. Telephone 01228 576579. Open: Mon - Fri 17.00 to midnight. Sat, Sun 12.00 to 01.00. Snacks at all times, hot meals: Fri, Sat 12.00 to 14.00 & 18.00 to 20.45.

Glasson

Highland Laddie. Telephone 016973 51839. Open: Weekdays 12.00 to midnight. Sat, Sun 12.00 to 01.00. Food served Mon - Sat 12.00 to 15.00 & 18.30 to 20.45. Sun 12.00 to 14.00 & 18.30 to 20.45. No food served on Tuesdays, telephone -to check availability.

Port Carlisle

Hope and Anchor. Telephone 016973 51460. Open Mon - Thur 12.00 to 23.00. Fri - Sat 12.00 to 12.00. Sunday 12.00 to 22.30. Food served: 12.00 to 15.00 & 18.00 to 21.00 daily except Mondays.

Bowness-on-Solway

The King's Arms. Telephone 016973 51426. Also passport stamping station. Open daily 11.00 to 23.00. Hot meals 12.00 to 14.00. Bar meals 18.00 to 21.00 daily except Wednesdays.

Notes

Notes